PROOF OF THE SUN
a memoir in verse

Proof of the Sun

Eve Ott

QUERENCIA

Querencia Press, LLC
Chicago Illinois

QUERENCIA PRESS

© Copyright 2024
Eve Ott

ISBN 978 1 959118 69 5

.
www.querenciapress.com

First Published in 2024

Querencia Press, LLC
Chicago IL

Printed & Bound in the United States of America

CONTENTS

Proof of the Sun chronicles my journey through childhood sexual abuse. It was painful, and as those who have walked a similar path know, it was long. But, once you walk through it and emerge, you know that the longest shadow merely proves the sun.

—Eve Ott, 2023

By the Sea

If a memory of childhood sexual abuse could be comic
here's how it would begin:

The women recline on the beach in their modest swimsuits,
his wife, his mother-in-law, and that sister-in-law,
mother of the little girl he now pulls through
the gentle waters of Long Island Sound.
He gives them a one-armed wave,
being careful to keep his other arm submerged.
The women smile, wave back—
          "Isn't he wonderful?"

to the Yale graduate who married one of their own
humble, but extraordinarily respectable,
Christmas, Easter, baptism, wedding, and funeral Episcopalian
family.
Look at that big, beautiful colonial style home he built for her
at the very top of the tall hill on the street that bears his name,
Look how he now displays his grace and generosity
by playing with that poor little girl of a far less fortunate
and, yes, less respectable family member.
Head-shakingly wonderful, that's what he is.

Mr. Wonderful zig-zags, causing the little girl's body
To twist and swish back and forth, back and forth.
She sputters and giggles.
and holds ever tighter to his cock.

Sun Block

The first time I was sent on the train
to spend the weekend with my aunt and uncle,

so my single mama could have a break for a change,

I was excited.

The conductor called me Little Lady
in a surprisingly soft and gentle voice
considering what a big man he was.
The sailor with the twinkling eyes
sitting across the aisle
gave me a playful wink.

When the train sighed into the next station
the conductor lifted me down to the platform
and delivered me in person to my Aunt and Uncle.

Auntie, who had no children of her own, was excited
and fussed over me in a voice a lot like Momma's.
Uncle stood silhouetted against the setting sun,
his arms crossed on his chest,
gazing down at me with one eyebrow arched,
as if he were inspecting a package
that might be damaged,
that he could damage.

I stood in his long, long shadow
wondering if he'd let me stay
or send me back.

When finally he pressed a bill into the conductor's
smooth, expectant palm,
I figured I'd passed.

Only later would I learn how long a shadow
one man could cast.

Once Upon a Time

Model it, baby, model it, he said.

Holding the long skirt
of my new nightie
and arching one arm
above my head.
I turned
on tip toe
before my aunt and uncle.

He threw his head back and roared
which stopped me in my tracks.

I must have done it wrong.

But then, as Auntie went to the kitchen,
he swept me up in his arms
and carried me upstairs,
his jewelry box ballerina,
lifted my pretty new nightie,
sat me in his lap,
unzipped,
and began my bedtime story.

Goodbye Dick, Goodbye Jane, Goodbye Funny, Funny Baby

How old was I when this story began?
I'm really not sure.
I remember that on my first train trip
all by myself, I was reading
a book about Dick and Jane

that, unbelievable as it may seem,
even to me,
I remember loving.

I loved Mother in her apron.
I loved Father in his suit.
I loved funny, funny baby.

Auntie wore an apron.
Uncle wore a suit.
In the mornings, I would watch Uncle shave.
In the evenings, I would wait on the front step
for him to return from work.
When his car pulled into the driveway,
I would race toward it.
He would put his briefcase down,
sweep one arm between my legs
and swing me up above his head
where I'd hang giggling.
Man, I had arrived!

So I guess I was 5 or 6.
I know I wasn't 8 yet.
By the time I was 8
I'd quit being a little girl.
But I remember loving.

The Patient Progression

He was exceptionally patient,
got to give him that.
In retrospect, the steps could be numbered.

1. Establish respect.
    No problem.
    Family did that for him,
    so educated, so wealthy,
    so honored to have a place at his Thanksgiving table,
    honored to gather round his Christmas Tree.
Number one: check

2. Build trust
    Be carried out beyond where your feet can touch.
    Lie on the water, his hands beneath your back.
    Do not panic when he draws them away.
    Don't sink. Don't drown. Breathe. Float.
    Number two: check

3. Become a pair, a club of two.
    "Bedtime is our time. Just us. No one else.
    We will read a story.
    "She tried the big bowl of porridge but it was—"
                "Too hot."
    I will stroke your hair as we read our story.
    "She sat on the middle sized chair but it was—"
                "Too soft."
    You will hold me here and move your hand like this.
    "She tried the little bed and it was—"
                "Just right!"

To Banbury Cross

Uncle came up with a new water game.

He called it "under water close together,"
a game in which he would put his penis inside
the crotch of my bathing suit so I could ride it
as we went down, down, down,
below where the jelly fish flashed
down to where crabs crawled rocks
a mirror
hung heavy with undulating seaweed.

Clues

A teenaged cousin visited.
She went swimming with me and Uncle.
I paddled over to Uncle.
Close together, close together, I said,
clasping my arms around his neck.

To my surprise, Uncle pushed me away.
With the backs of his hands
he splashed water in my face.

He and the cousin exchanged looks,
his, wide-eyed, eyebrows arched in surprise,
hers, mouth-puckered amusement,
a look that totally excluded me.

Climax

After the cousin left,
the games resumed,
of course they did,
including under water close together.

This time Uncle clasped me tighter as we sank,
then tighter and even tighter,
one arm around my back,
one hand holding my bottom.
And then

he peed on me.
What else could that warm fluid
pulsing into the crotch of my swim suit be?
He peed on me.

How could he?
                How could he?
                                How could he?

Turning Point

Mama said she had a terrible headache.
She said she had to lie down
and I had to leave her alone for awhile.

That wasn't unusual.
Mama frequently had headaches
and lay on the bed with a cloth over her eyes.

I made no connection to the fact
I had just told her Uncle had peed,
not in his pants
but in mine.

Mama arose with red-rimmed, very sad eyes.
She motioned to me to come sit with her in our rocker.

She looked at me long and hard.
What Uncle did was very bad, she said.

Well, yes. I already knew that.
Who wouldn't?

You must never ever tell anyone
what you told me today, she continued.

If Auntie ever knew—what he did—
it would kill her, do you understand?

No. I did not understand.
What did any of it have to do with Auntie?
And if it was Uncle who did something bad,
why was I suddenly feeling at fault?

Do you understand? She repeated,
in her I-mean-business voice.

Yes. I said. But that was a lie.
No. I did not understand.

Attempted Therapy

Some time later, Mama took me downtown.
She said she had errands to run
but I could stay in one of those big college buildings
where some very nice people would take care of me.

Holding my hand, she led me into the big building.
We sat in a room with lots of chairs
until the smiley lady came to meet us.
She led us to another room

where there was a small chair and a low table
on which sat the most beautiful doll house
I had ever seen, and lined up next to it
an entire little family.

Mama kissed my cheek and waved goodbye.
I'll be back soon, she said.
Before the smiley lady even told me I could,
I began placing the tiny figures in the doll house.

I'll be in the next room, she said,
gesturing to an open door next to
a long, mirrored wall.
I nodded, already engrossed in play.

The furniture in the house was so perfect,
A stove in the kitchen, a sofa with cushions in the living room.
There were even toys in a room for the little girl
and her brother to play with.
And there was a crib for the baby.

After a time the lady with the smile came back.

She pulled up a chair next to mine.
Tell me about your family, she said.
Even her voice was smiley.

I showed her Mama in her Kitchen.
I showed her Sister pushing her doll carriage.
I showed her Brother and his toy truck,
and Baby sleeping in her crib.

Where's the father, she asked.
I looked around the table.
There, I said, pointing, when I'd spotted him.

Years later I learned Mama had left me
at the famed Gesell Institute of Child Psychology.
I don't remember how many sessions there were.
I remember only the one, but no matter how many,
I am certain they never got anything out of me
about Uncle and his water games.
Perhaps Mama should have held off
on swearing me to secrecy?

Attempted Therapy 2

After Uncle'd taught me
the difference between love and manipulation,
between an exclusive club and a cabal,
the first thing I did was cut off the curls
Mama kept me coiffed in.
I had to wear skirts to school,
but the rest of the time,
strictly Levis and tees or sweatshirts for me.
It took me awhile to break in
but eventually I ran
with the neighborhood boys,
shunning the budding girls.
I wanted to be Tom Sawyer,
be Huckleberry Finn, be Robinson Crusoe,
not just read about them.
Who would ever want to be just a girl
when boys had all the adventures, all the fun?

I know my behavior upset Mama,
heavily invested as she was in having
a sweet, pretty girl with curls.
I'm sorry, Mama,
but that door was locked.
Still, Uncle may have taught me
some very important life lessons.
Too early, to be sure,
but important, nonetheless.

Attempted Therapy 3:

An Unexpected Gift

It wasn't my birthday
It wasn't Christmas,
but Mama suddenly bought me
that little 10-foot rowboat
I'd begged for all year.
Even more surprising,
it came with permission
to go out in it anytime I wanted to.

I would often awake at dawn,
pull on shorts and a tee,
Run barefoot down the hill,
across Ocean Avenue,
and scramble down the rocks to the shore
where my beloved 10-foot rowboat
was anchored.

If it was low tide,
I'd have to push and pull my little craft
across the sandbar to the water's edge,
run back for the anchor,
then shove off into the sound.

If high tide,
I'd have to swim night-chilled waters
out to where my boat bobbed.

Then I'd fit the oars in the oarlocks
And row.
Plish, splash, plish, splash

At low tide I'd end up
very far from the shore .
Plish, splash, plish, splash.
Less so if high,
Plish, splash, plish.

When the shore looked just a line,
nothing more,
I'd pull the oars in,
lean back,
and drift.
the tide swelled,
rolled in,
broke on the shore,
inhaled,
and did it again,
again,
again.

A Belief in forgiveness

Mama had it in spades
So, after a brief time of made up excuses
for our absence at family gatherings
we returned.

I did not know about forgiveness,
or condemnation.
I didn't even know for sure
what was good and what was evil.

I did know I did not want to go back
to that big house on the hill.

I did not want to go on Christmas Eve,
which happened also to be my birthday.
I did not want to choke down another piece
of Grandmother's famous fruit cake
someone had stuck a candle in.
But that's what I did.

I did not want to go there on Christmas day,
open presents and coo over their contents
whether I liked them or not.
But that's what I did.

I did not want to go on 4th of July
when we might go swimming.
But that's what I did.

I didn't want to see Auntie, over whose life
I apparently held such terrifying power,
and I definitely didn't want to see that—guy

But that's what I did,
year after year after year
until the year I left home
which was the first year that I possibly could.

But Mama Did Know Best

When my marriage to my first husband was running aground,
we went to marriage counseling,
individual, couple, and group.
In one of the individual sessions
I told the counselor about Uncle and me.
Now that got his attention!
Questions, questions, questions.
When our session was concluding he said:
It's amazing to me how many of the women I see
have had similar experiences.

I could have told him how many of the women I saw,
at coffees, at PTA meetings, at church, for cryin' out loud,
had had similar experiences too,
but I was too stunned
by his clear implication
that the problem in my marriage was me.
I was simply too messed up
for a happy relationship,
a conclusion my then-husband
completely concurred with.

I never should have told either of them.

But What No One Talks About Ever

Is this:
After all the pump priming beforehand,
so to speak,

all that lifting up
of the fatherless girl—

(most of us are fatherless girls,
unless it's the old man himself.)

what ev—

We're left
awakened in the predawn

never able
to escape the unspeakable knowledge

that the pleasure
was not
all
his.

And That's the Way It Goes

Being sexually abused as a child
flips a switch that cannot be turned off.

And this,
not the pain, not the betrayal, not the humiliation,
causes the most enduring damage.

Despite
running with the boys, dressing like the boys,
I also flirted with the boys,
sometimes outrageously.

I was—
not a slut.

I was—
as Idealistic as they come.

I wanted
"true love"
I wanted
fidelity.
Someday
I wanted to get married and stay married
Till death should part us,
but

I was also completely cockeyed.

I know for sure
I could have been knocked up
at age fourteen had my boyfriend

not loved me enough
to push me away.
So I left him
for those who loved me less.

I know for sure
that's why I married my first husband.
And let's get real here,
my second, too.
Cockeyed.

But
if that alarm
awakens you,
there's no going back to sleep.
No matter how early it might be.
you just have to get up,
run down to the shore,
and row out far enough
to see the humor
in highly respectable ladies
smiling adoringly
at a wealthy and powerful man
pulling an innocently giggling little girl
through the water
by his cock;

far enough to know
the shadow
proves
the sun.

Notes on Previous Publications

<u>Gimme Your Luch Money</u> - "Once Upon a Time" appeared as
"Bedtime Story"

Milton Keynes UK
Ingram Content Group UK Ltd.
UKHW041835091223
433957UK00017B/248